This ————

BOLD AND EASY

Coloring book belongs to:

Island Smiles Press

BOLD AND EASY LARGE PRINT COLORING BOOK

TEST YOUR COLORS

Try out your pens and pencils in these circle guides to see how the colors look on the paper before you begin. To help avoid bleed-through we have added grey tints on the reverse side of each coloring page. If you are using markers try inserting a thicker piece of paper or cardboard behind the page you are coloring to protect the page behind. Happy coloring!

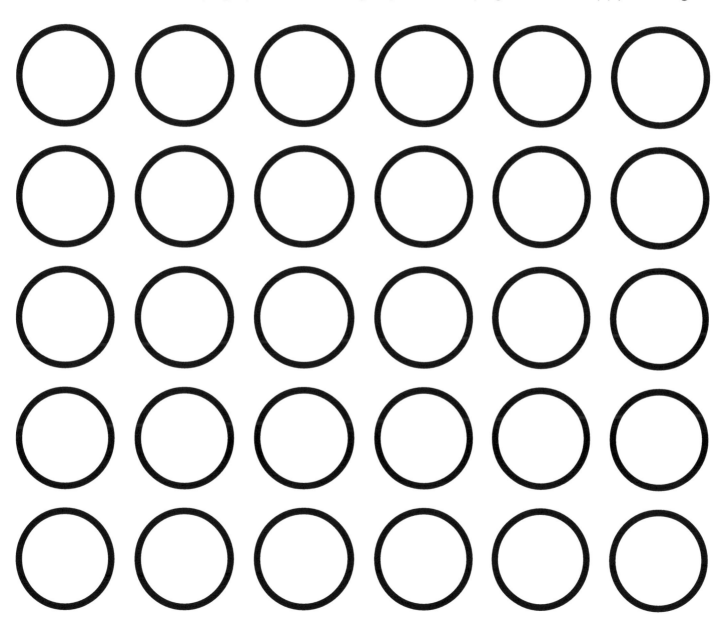

BOLD AND EASY LARGE PRINT COLORING BOOK

BOLD AND EASY LARGE PRINT COLORING BOOK

BOLD AND EASY LARGE PRINT COLORING BOOK

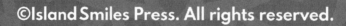

BOLD AND EASY LARGE PRINT COLORING BOOK

BOLD AND EASY LARGE PRINT COLORING BOOK

BOLD AND EASY LARGE PRINT COLORING BOOK

BOLD AND EASY LARGE PRINT COLORING BOOK

BOLD AND EASY LARGE PRINT COLORING BOOK

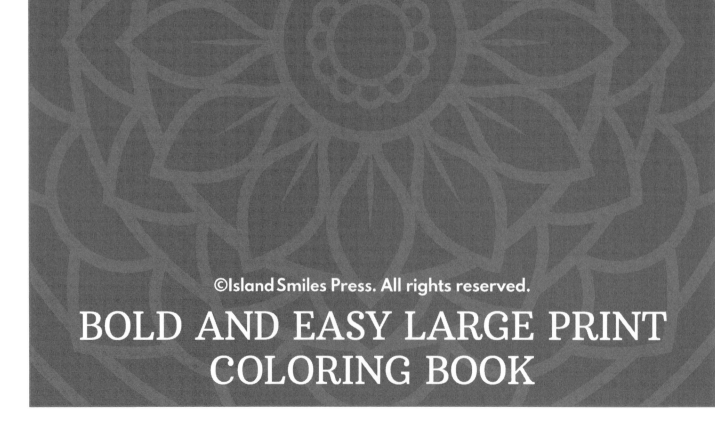

BOLD AND EASY LARGE PRINT COLORING BOOK

BOLD AND EASY LARGE PRINT COLORING BOOK

BOLD AND EASY LARGE PRINT COLORING BOOK

BOLD AND EASY LARGE PRINT
COLORING BOOK

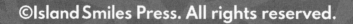

BOLD AND EASY LARGE PRINT COLORING BOOK

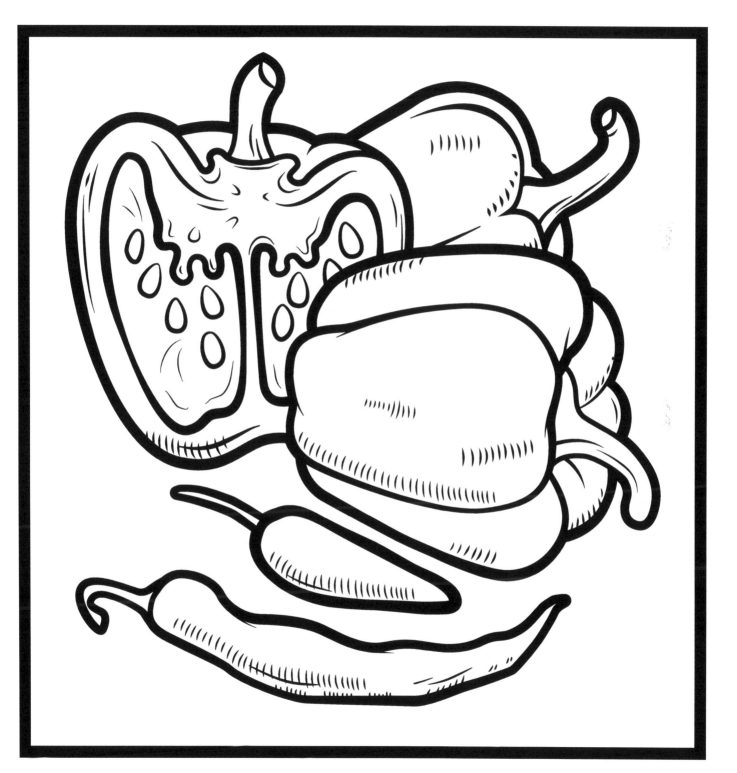

BOLD AND EASY LARGE PRINT
COLORING BOOK

BOLD AND EASY LARGE PRINT COLORING BOOK

BOLD AND EASY LARGE PRINT COLORING BOOK

BOLD AND EASY LARGE PRINT COLORING BOOK

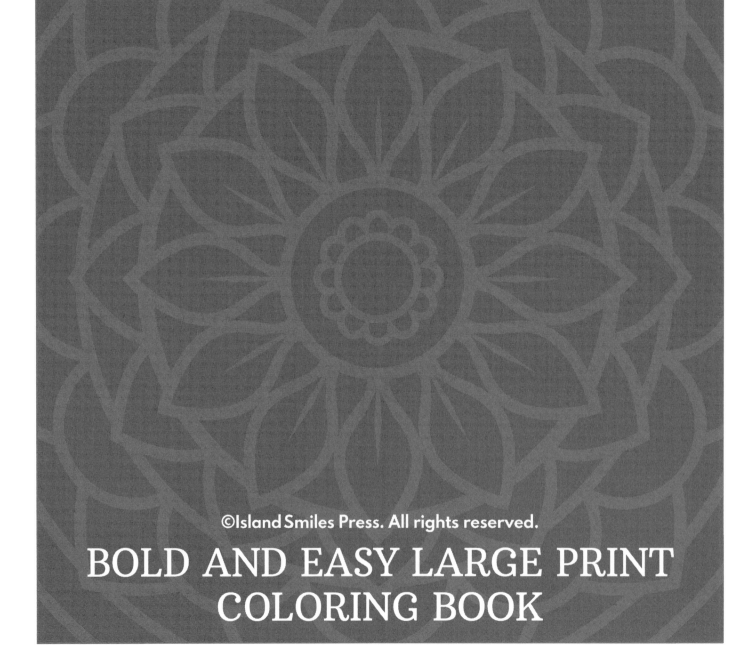

BOLD AND EASY LARGE PRINT
COLORING BOOK

BOLD AND EASY LARGE PRINT COLORING BOOK

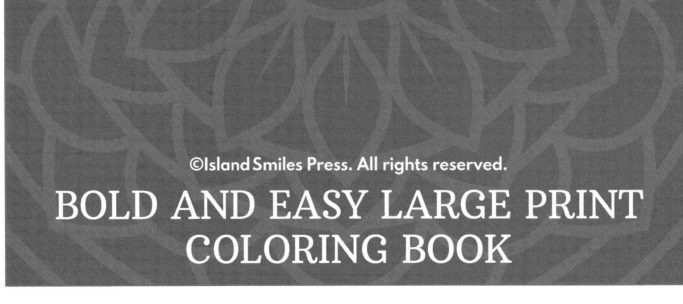

BOLD AND EASY LARGE PRINT COLORING BOOK

BOLD AND EASY LARGE PRINT COLORING BOOK

BOLD AND EASY LARGE PRINT COLORING BOOK

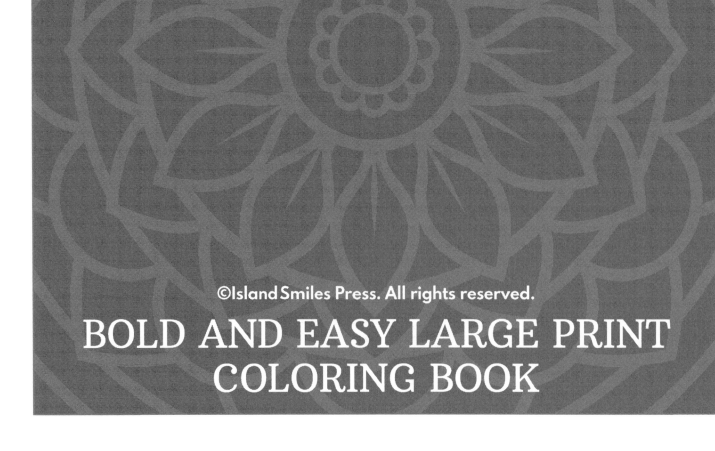

BOLD AND EASY LARGE PRINT
COLORING BOOK

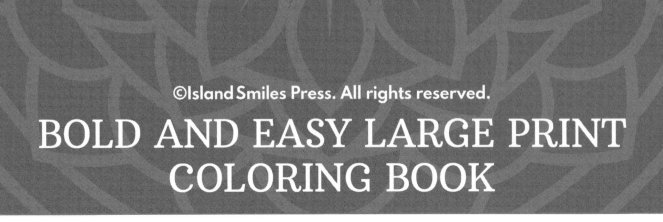

BOLD AND EASY LARGE PRINT
COLORING BOOK

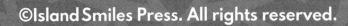

BOLD AND EASY LARGE PRINT
COLORING BOOK

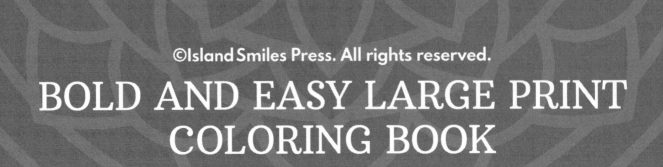

BOLD AND EASY LARGE PRINT
COLORING BOOK

BOLD AND EASY LARGE PRINT COLORING BOOK

BOLD AND EASY LARGE PRINT
COLORING BOOK

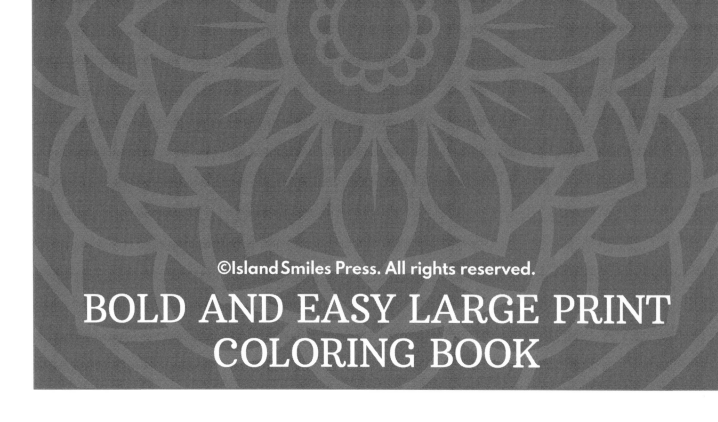

BOLD AND EASY LARGE PRINT
COLORING BOOK

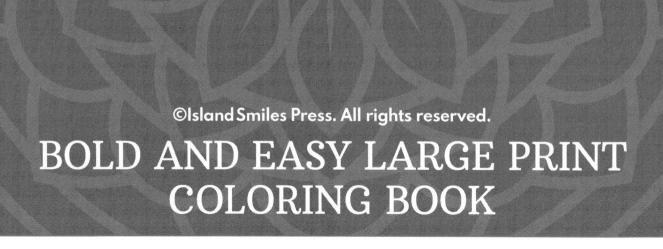

BOLD AND EASY LARGE PRINT COLORING BOOK

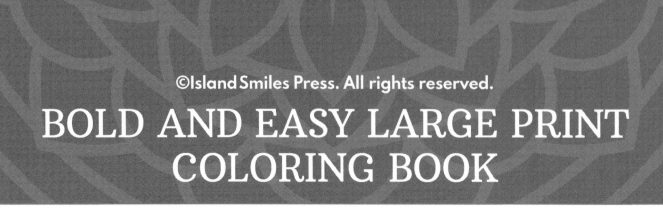

BOLD AND EASY LARGE PRINT COLORING BOOK

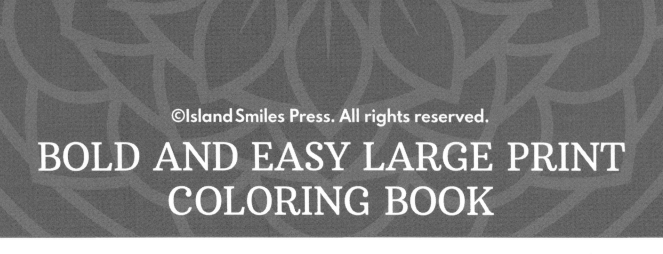

BOLD AND EASY LARGE PRINT COLORING BOOK

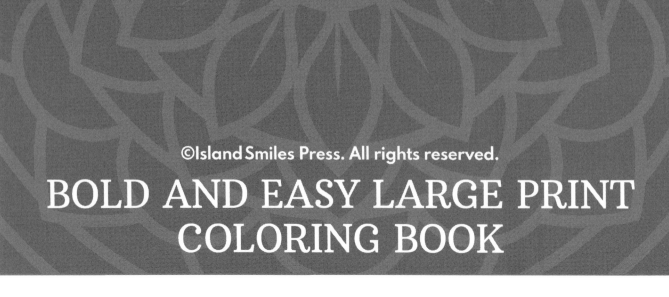

BOLD AND EASY LARGE PRINT
COLORING BOOK

BOLD AND EASY LARGE PRINT
COLORING BOOK

BOLD AND EASY LARGE PRINT
COLORING BOOK

BOLD AND EASY LARGE PRINT
COLORING BOOK

BOLD AND EASY LARGE PRINT
COLORING BOOK

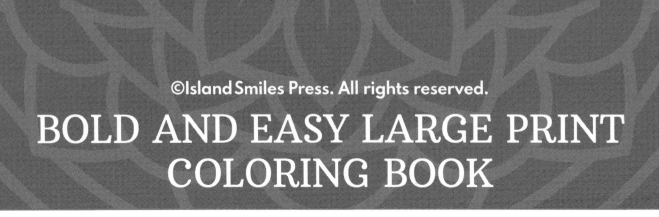

BOLD AND EASY LARGE PRINT COLORING BOOK

BOLD AND EASY LARGE PRINT COLORING BOOK

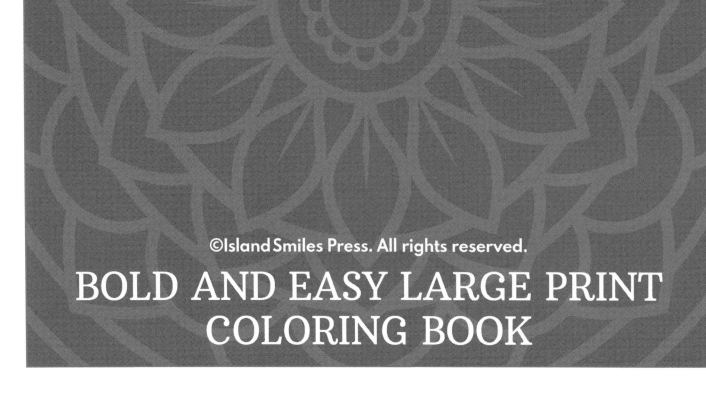

BOLD AND EASY LARGE PRINT COLORING BOOK

BOLD AND EASY LARGE PRINT COLORING BOOK

Made in the USA
Coppell, TX
14 October 2023

22829540R00048